Clara Porset
Butaque

ANA ELENA MALLET

THE MUSEUM OF MODERN ART, NEW YORK

Clara Porset (Mexican, born Cuba. 1895–1981). Butaque. c. 1957. Laminated wood and woven wicker, 28 ¾ × 25 ¹³⁄₁₆ × 33 ⁷⁄₁₆" (73 × 65.6 × 84.9 cm). THE MUSEUM OF MODERN ART. GIFT OF THE MODERN WOMEN'S FUND

FIG. 1. Clara Porset with a butaque, c. 1955

IN HER 1949 ARTICLE "¿QUÉ ES DISEÑO?" (WHAT IS DESIGN?), PUBLISHED IN THE popular magazine *Arquitectura México*, designer Clara Porset [**FIG. 1**] set forth a credo regarding her field. Hers was an ample vision: "In everything, there is design," she wrote, "in a cloud, in a fingerprint, on the sand or in the sea, set in motion by the wind. It is also present in a chair, a glass, a weaving. It can be natural or human-made, but there is design in everything we perceive."[1] She returned to these words in the catalogue of the exhibition *El arte en la vida diaria: Exposición de objetos de buen diseño hechos en México* (Art in Daily Life: Exhibition of Well-Designed Objects Made in Mexico), which she organized in 1952. The show presented the public with an ideal version of daily life, implemented through exceptional objects derived from popular culture, along with products of the nascent industries of furniture, textiles, ceramics, and metalwork.

As early as the 1930s, drawing on criteria derived from avant-garde aesthetics, The Museum of Modern Art in New York had formulated a series of precepts to help consumers distinguish between "good" and "bad" (or well-designed and poorly designed) commercial objects.[2] Porset took this notion a step further, identifying *taste* as a necessary component in understanding modern art and design. Relatedly, she believed that artisans were essential to the expressive potentials of design, which she felt ought to characterize the transition to industrialism—as opposed to functionalism's stark, formalist orientation. And yet, in Porset's exhibition wall text for *El arte en la vida diaria*, she asserted: "A machine-made form is no less beautiful than a handmade one," signaling her vision of the shift toward a utopian modern lifestyle linked to its surroundings, where consumption, identity, progress, and popular art are all mediated by design [**FIG. 2**].

FIG. 2. Installation view of *El arte en la vida diaria: Exposición de objetos de buen diseño hechos en México,* Ciudad Universitaria, Universidad Nacional Autónoma de México (UNAM), Mexico City, 1952

Throughout her career, in search of localized examples of "expressive design," Porset turned to pieces of vernacular furniture that, reinterpreted through modern paradigms, became icons of her own design production. The *butaque* is without question her most emblematic piece [**FIGS. 3–5**]. This low, curved chair, with its wooden structure and seat traditionally made of animal skin, reflects the idiosyncrasies of the several Latin American regions from which it derives. The classic butaque dates back to at least the sixteenth century; it includes functional design elements introduced by the Spanish conquistadores with modifications made to meet the conditions of new geographies, climates, and natural resources. As such, the butaque is a hybrid piece that sums up the heritage, material wealth, and profound cultural interchanges between two civilizations.

Porset understood the butaque as a regional typology, which she reworked and adapted to modern interiors. The chair, reread through her eyes, was used by distinguished architects of Mexican modernity in order to bring a sense of visual harmony to their interiors. She was not alone in this re-envisioning: the butaque typology was taken up by a number of Latin American designers of the twentieth and twenty-first centuries, in order to propose questions about culture, identity, locale, and territorial presence. Porset's investigations into its role and meanings were among the most thorough.

A TRAINING IN DESIGN

Porset was born in Matanzas, Cuba, in 1895, but spent crucial periods of her life in Mexico; today she is considered a fundamental reference point for Mexican design. As a professional and a pioneer in her field, she challenged the social conventions of her time and succeeded in distinguishing herself as an interior designer during what is often termed the "heroic period" of modern Mexican design—from the 1940s to the 1970s—during which industrialization flourished in the country, opening new possibilities for designers.

Porset came from a wealthy Cuban family. Her mother, Clara del Rosario Dumas y Franco, was a native of Cienfuegos, on the island's southern coast. Her father, Adolfo Porset, was the civil governor of Matanzas during the final years of Spanish colonization. Clara's privileged status enabled her to study abroad, in the United States and France. During her adolescence, between 1911 and 1914, she attended New York's Manhattanville College of the Sacred Heart, a liberal arts school for young women. Later, around 1925, she studied art, architecture, and design at Columbia University's department of fine arts and at the New York School of Interior Decoration. Between 1927 and 1929 she resumed her architectural and design studies, now in Paris: first at the Sorbonne and subsequently in the studio of the distinguished architect Henri Rapin.[3]

FIG. 3. Clara Porset. Butaque, side view

FIGS. 4, 5. Clara Porset. Butaque, rear view and detail

Upon her return to Cuba in 1929, Porset became involved with various groups of artists and intellectuals who were opposed to the regime of the country's president, Gerardo Machado. Between 1931 and 1933, she contributed to the journal *Social*, founded in 1916 by publisher and political cartoonist Conrado Walter Massaguer [**FIG. 6**]. The publication was an important resource for a generation of youth with democratic ideals, embracing modernist aesthetics but also driven to blaze new political and social paths in Cuba. In addition, it was a publishing platform for the anti-imperialist Grupo Minorista, with which Porset had close ties.[4]

During her years in Cuba, along with attending fashion shows and other events among Cuban high society, Porset was a frequent visitor to the Lyceum de La Habana, a women's cultural center founded in 1929.[5] The Lyceum promoted the interchange of ideas and the social and intellectual training of middle- and upper-class Cuban women through courses, lectures, cultural programs, and exhibitions. A number of the artists and intellectuals associated with the Minorista movement (many of whom also contributed to *Social*) frequented the Lyceum. Here Porset would surely have mingled with the Cuban cultural elite, but it was likely also at the Lyceum that she began to explore the socialist ideas that would later lead her to abandon her country and that, once she was in Mexico, would contribute to the development of her own singular design project.[6]

In 1932 Porset, virulently opposed to the Machado regime, went into voluntary exile in New York; there she became informally involved with the Cuban revolutionary junta, which had headquarters in the city.[7] In the United States, she became notorious (as reported in various national newspapers) for her denunciation of the censorship and harassment inflicted upon activist women like herself.[8] In 1933, after the fall of the Machado government, Porset returned to Cuba and was appointed lecturer and director of the industrial arts program at Havana's Escuela Técnica Industrial "Fundación Rosalía Abreu," a technical college for economically disadvantaged Cuban women from rural backgrounds. While putting together her study program, and as part of her research for the school's curriculum, she traveled to North Carolina in the summer of 1934 to spend a few weeks at Black Mountain College, in an effort to understand the bold educational model implemented there by the German artist Josef Albers. Albers and his wife, artist and designer Anni Albers, both of whom had been at the Bauhaus, had arrived at Black Mountain College upon its founding the previous year. This was Porset's first contact with the Alberses, who would become her close friends; they shared artistic as well as political interests, in matters of design and research into art and arts education. Porset initiated the Alberses' long relationship with Latin America by inviting Josef to give a series of lectures at Havana's Lyceum, first in 1934, and again the following year. Later in 1935 she

FIG. 6. Cover of *Social* magazine, September 1931

would host them in Mexico, along with their friends Theodore and Barbara Dreier [**FIG. 7**]. It was the first of the Alberses' many trips to the country: they would travel to Mexico no fewer than a dozen times between this visit and their last, in 1967.

In 1935, following her participation in the Cuban general strike, Porset was fired from her position at the Escuela Técnica and forced again into exile. This time she was drawn to Mexico, now under the administration of President Lázaro Cárdenas, a popular leftist reformer. For Porset, this displacement became a journey of opportunities and resulted in the construction of a design project based on patrimony, history, and tradition—a project that she would later bring back to her country of birth.

FIG. 7. From left: Clara Porset, Theodore and Barbara Dreier, and Anni Albers, 1934–35. Photo: Josef Albers

MEXICO: HOME FOR AN EXILE

Porset arrived in Mexico in 1936. The nation's political system was undergoing a profound transformation that came in the wake of the Mexican Revolution (1910–1917). After that conflict, the country's reconstruction was engaged with a unifying mission to recognize and celebrate a national identity, of which the return to the vernacular and to Indigenous cultures was a central symbolic directive.[9]

Porset's experience working in Cuba and her time abroad had taught her that, in matters of industrial design, Latin American realities—its conditions, materials, heritage, and cultural and political issues—were decidedly different from those of other parts of the world. Mexico enabled her to be a pioneer and to develop as a designer, as well as to venture into other fields fostered by the period's incipient culture of design: writing, teaching, organizing exhibitions, and promoting design as a discipline. The first job Porset held in Mexico, in 1936–37, was as a temporary replacement for the poet Carlos Pellicer, as chair of the art history program at the Universidad Nacional Autónoma de México's summer school. The newly arrived designer soon joined the Liga de Escritores y Artistas Revolucionarios (LEAR: League of Revolutionary Writers and Artists), an organization run by artists, writers, and architects involved in political activities that opposed the imperialist and fascist currents threatening the world at that time. It was in this milieu that Porset built a circle of friendships and political connections with other artists and intellectuals, exchanging ideas and opinions on design and architecture and their role in the postrevolutionary context.

Porset's interest in Indigenous Mexican culture, popular arts and crafts, and the rural villages where they were produced was profoundly influenced by the artist Xavier Guerrero, one of her colleagues in the LEAR, whom she married in 1938.[10] Guerrero was a member of the Mexican Communist Party and one of the founding members of the postrevolutionary Mexican Muralist movement. He was also a collector and enthusiast of popular arts, as well as having been trained in carpentry and furniture construction [FIG. 8].

In their first years together, Porset collaborated with Guerrero on several projects. In 1941 they participated in the "Organic Design in Home Furnishings" competition convened by MoMA in New York—the first such event to include Latin American designers. The competition had two categories: one for the United States, in which such designers as Eero Saarinen and Charles Eames participated, and another for Latin America. The response to MoMA's invitation was enthusiastic: proposals came in from seventeen countries in Latin America alone. The Museum's general intention with the competition was to stimulate production, new materials, and local output during wartime, as well as to energize the US market. The Latin American participants were, however, oriented more toward using local materials from territories to the south. Porset and Guerrero presented an ensemble that they termed "rural furniture

FIG. 8. Xavier Guerrero, Clara Porset, and their dog "Pedrito," n.d.

setting" [FIG. 9]. The simple furnishings, made of pinewood and natural fibers—materials common throughout most of Mexico—moved the jury to award them the prize. Although they signed the work as a duo, and Porset was the only woman taking part in the competition, it was Guerrero who traveled to New York to receive the prize. Nonetheless, this success would serve as a stimulus for the couple's more experimental collaborations in the following years.[11]

———

Over the following decades, Porset remained in Mexico and dedicated herself to translating the vision of the Mexican Revolution's political and cultural project into utilitarian objects for daily use with a modern focus, while also taking into account the local social climate and material conditions. These years of continuous employment were productive and encouraging for the designer. While there were certainly moments when her work and contributions went unrecognized, over time she succeeded in making a name for herself and a space within which to collaborate with the most distinguished architects of Mexican modernism: Alberto T. Arai, Luis Barragán, Max Ludwig Cetto, Juan Sordo Madaleno, Mario Pani, and Enrique Yáñez, among others.

FIG. 9. Installation view of *Organic Design in Home Furnishings*, The Museum of Modern Art, New York, 1941

Her work was focused both on the creation of furniture and on projects of "interior design"—a term she preferred to "interior decoration," as she found "design" to be a more apt designation.[12] Indeed, throughout her professional life, Porset made a point of avoiding the word "decoration," which was, she felt, associated with (and thus disdained as) women's work; the word "design," by contrast, established a certain neutrality not associated with gender. It may go without saying that, in that era, being a woman in the arena of design (or "decoration")—and indeed everything related to femininity—had its inconvenient aspects, as evidenced even at the most prestigious institutions, including the Bauhaus.

Porset's position, as an interior designer with a strong inclination toward a national style, was unique in Mexico at that time. Other professionals were accustomed to developing their work within the framework of "decoration," as was the case with Luisa P. de Guieu and her Elite studio, or with Arturo Pani (brother of the distinguished architect Mario Pani), a champion of eclectic interiors who often combined classic European antiquities and artful furnishings evoking historical styles. Determined to establish herself on the scene, Porset traveled to remote areas of Mexico to observe and investigate the domestic utensils and furnishings used in rural communities. In her 1948 article "Folk Furniture of Mexico," she analyzed a series of pieces of Mexican rural furniture, explaining their uses, forms, and materials.[13] The analysis considers everyday objects such as *xicapextle* (gourds) from the city of Tehuantepec, stools for milking cows, woven mats, as well as items with more elaborate processes of fabrication, like boxes from Olinalá, chairs from Tenancingo, *equipales* (traditional low seats made of wicker and leather) from Nayarit, and more. In this text, Porset stresses the importance of the popular and everything associated with the word "folk," a term with important symbolic weight, which had gained currency in the 1920s. She adopted a nationalist discourse, which she understood as protective of artisanal processes that were at risk due to industrialization, the displacements of rural populations to the city, and other phenomena, including the "vogue of things Mexican" abroad that was helping the market to thrive, as well as the proliferation of charlatan dealers in false folklore and Mexican curios.[14] Porset was by no means opposed to industrialization—she saw it as an indispensable tool of forward motion and development—but she emphasized the importance of maintaining manual labor and preserving the authenticity of handmade objects. As part of her argument, she declared that vernacular Mexican furniture, especially seating, was mestizo—that is, a product of the fusion of two cultural sources: Indigenous and Spanish. In "Folk Furniture of Mexico," she explained that popular art had been the means of expression for generations of creative artisans with unique aesthetic and imaginative capacities. Likewise, she discussed the ways in which mechanical progress and handcraft traditions could generate products with added value and an identity reflective of a modern Mexico.[15]

Porset's own designs for furniture were defined not only by their process of production with traditional materials, but also by their accommodations for geographic and climatic conditions. She believed that tropical environments required armchairs and hammocks in "free, airy, almost horizontal" positions, unlike the more upright chairs of the cooler North. Further, she maintained that these pieces' traditional forms had been determined by a variety of historical and identitarian assumptions. In the same 1948 article, Porset considered the emphasis that Spanish conquistadores placed on the relative lowness of Aztec emperor Montezuma's chairs, noting that the presence of the traditional *petates* (woven bedrolls) and three-legged stools had long determined "the reduced height of the seats" as well as "the scarcity of furnishings in [Mexican] interiors."[16] Seating oneself is not a mere physical act, Porset pointed out; it is a gesture that encodes the culture as a whole. These ideas are the basis for the development of an important part of her theoretical discourse and were reflected in her subsequent writings as well as in her lectures, classes, and design projects.

People in the United States had long been curious about their neighbor to the south, but in the 1940s, with the war in Europe limiting travel possibilities, Mexico had become an almost obligatory destination for many, and interest in the country's cultural riches intensified.[17] In February 1947 the *New York Times* reviewed an exhibition of a furniture set designed by Porset at Artek-Pascoe, Alvar and Aino Aalto's design store in midtown Manhattan.[18] These furnishings were far removed from what had previously been considered "Mexican": with their artisanal touches, they offered a breath of fresh air. The ensemble, proposed for a small one-bedroom apartment, consisted of five basic items made of cedar. The piece that most attracted public attention—as the *Times* writer put it, "the one piece that clearly betrays its Mexican heritage"—was the classic butaque. For Porset, the butaque reflected honesty of the materials, a connection to rural roots and to the historical past. She considered it a piece with its own aesthetic approach that, on the basis of its form and materials, was related to culture, tradition, and territory.

———

The butaque, although it has many variants, generally adheres to certain structural conventions. The word "butaque" designates a low chair with a curved structure made of wood and a seat of animal skin [**FIG. 10**]. Art historian Jorge Rivas Pérez, who has delved deep into the history of this chair, observes that the piece first emerged in Cumaná, Venezuela, toward the end of the sixteenth century, and borrows elements of the pre-Columbian chairs known as *duhos* as well as from the X-form folding chairs that the Spanish conquistadores brought to the Americas.[19] The first known mentions of butaques in Mexico date back to early cargo manifests in the states of Campeche and Veracruz. The former

Butaque de Teh

Un paso en la ev

butaque

Se supone que fué traído por los españoles, pero ha sido tal su asimilación a la vida mexicana que actualmente puede considerarse como una expresión popular nacional y, por ello, recibe el interés de algunos diseñadores que se preocupan por desarrollarlo.

Otra etapa de la evolución del butaque de Tehuantepec Diseño de CLARA PORSET

FIG. 10. Spread from the exhibition catalogue *El arte en la vida diaria: Exposición de objetos de buen diseño hechos en México* (Mexico City: Instituto Nacional de Bellas Artes, 1952)

FIG. 11. Unknown designer. Butaque armchair. 1780–1820. Campeche, Mexico. Spanish cedar, leather, and metal, 36¼ × 27½ × 28¾" (92.1 × 69.9 × 73 cm). DENVER ART MUSEUM. FUNDS FROM THE CARL PATTERSON BEQUEST

became a center of production and export of this chair, on account of which it was occasionally called the "Campeche chair" **[FIG. 11]**. Indeed, there are several versions of butaques in different parts of Latin America, each adapted to geographic and climatic conditions and available materials.

In the butaque, Porset recognized a design that reflected Mexico's complex national identity. Her research enabled her to understand the structural characteristics of the chair: how the curvature of the legs is achieved by working with the wood, how the seat and support are engineered with small planks, which cause less waste, and are joined very securely thanks to the large contact surface among the parts. She observed that the continuous curve integrating seat and support is a central design element that, if poorly handled, affects comfort and ease of use. She experimented with varying the structure's dimensions and the

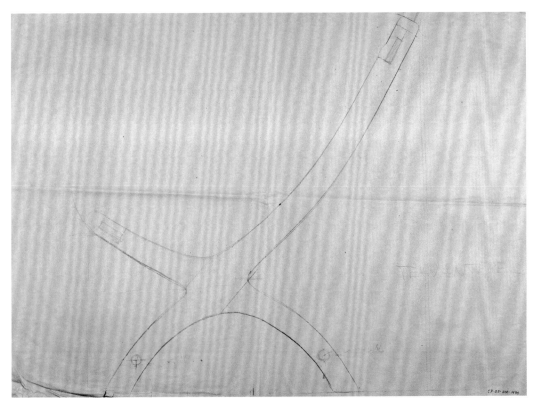

FIG. 12. Clara Porset (Mexican, born Cuba. 1895–1981). Side-view drawing of a Tehuantepec butaque. Graphite pencil on paper, 27½ × 39⅜" (70 × 100 cm). ARCHIVO CLARA PORSET DUMAS, CENTRO DE INVESTIGACIONES DE DISEÑO INDUSTRIAL, FACULTAD DE ARQUITECTURA, UNAM

seat's material. She tested a large range of textures with different fabrics and animal skins. Over the course of several years, she concentrated on these analyses of the butaque's structure in order to modify it, and through this process tried out a variety of proportions, finishes, and structural procedures **[FIG. 12]**. Ultimately, following this intensive investigation into the traditional butaque and its many uses in different contexts, Porset made ergonomic adjustments and adapted the dimensions of the chair to modern ideals of comfort and beauty.

While the great diversity of furnishings made by Porset is well known, chairs were a particular formal and conceptual preoccupation within her production. This is evidenced by the article she published in 1951 in the prestigious US magazine *Arts & Architecture*. In "Chairs by Clara Porset" **[FIG. 13]**, the designer lays out the goals of her work and declares that her production is known for

CHAIRS BY CLARA PORSET

In the developing of the "butaque," the first object was to eliminate the high crown and baroque curve yet retain its gracious lines. The chair is in leather and mahogany and also in mahogany and webbing.

Above and left, wicker seats for the garden of Enrique de la Mora. Designed first as a rocking chair; without rockers it becomes a garden seat.

My furniture is said to have a Mexican character. If so, it is a natural result of the objectives I seek; for I design chiefly for Mexicans and strive to produce shapes, as adequate as I may, for their specific conditions of living and their active needs which are also specific.

Practically all of my furniture is made by hand. And this—which is symptomatic of the present stage of the general process of production, still with a larger percentage of manual technique—is perhaps one of the principal factors that determine the special appearance of our forms. The method has inducement not only because of the quality of construction permitted by the skill of the craftsmen who collaborate in it, but it also has limitations. The use of the furniture is restricted by its inevitable high cost.

Most of the natural materials—webbing of palm, hemp, tule and ixtle—are exclusive to Mexico, and accentuate the regional and national imprint of the designs.

Furthermore, the average Mexican is clearly differentiated anatomically and has also distinctive cultural habits. These characteristics have their derivations in the form and use of the furniture requiring express shapes and employment. The BUTAQUE* and the EQUIPAL**—two old types that persist in use—show this well. They have such physical fitness for the user, and so subtle an affinity for his culture, that both can be held as prototypes of the popular furniture that is best adapted to the Mexicans. I have given a great deal of attention to the development of the butaque, and the demand for the type that I produce proves once more its original merit.

In addition to the already mentioned sources that give particular substance to the shapes belonging to Mexico, there is the extraordinary plastic heritage, whose reverberations are perceived constantly by those of us concerned with design in Mexico making us more aware of its moving forces.

And then I ask, if what I attempt to do in design is achieved, even partly, could it have any other character but Mexican?—CLARA PORSET GUERRERO.

*BUTAQUE—Mexican term derived from the Spanish butaca, used for a type of chair that may have originated in Egypt or in Spain, but wholly assimilated in Mexico.

**EQUIPAL—Modern term given to a type of chair originally Mexican and called icpalli, a sort of wooden throne used by high dignitaries.

Left and below in group, rush and pine furniture designed for government-sponsored housing project: Multi-Familiar. These are the lowest cost chairs in Mexico—38 pesos or $4.11.

Although most work in Mexico is manual, the Mexican is quite capable of understanding the machine, and as industries grow his facility in the use of the machine grows.

In Clara Porset's present task of searching throughout Mexico for material for an exhibit of Objects of Good Design, she finds an abundance of good machine-made objects.

Her experience in a small factory is that craftsmen may at first wish to conceal defective work with ornament but as their taste and conscience develop they take the same pride in machine work as they formerly did in hand work.

The furniture for the children's waiting room at Ratha Hospital, and, commissioned by the government, the development of low-cost furniture for a housing project are two design assignments recently completed. She assembled the material for the exhibition of modern Mexican architecture at the Palace of Fine Arts this spring.

Clara Porset is married to Xavier Guerrero, the muralist. They once collaborated on a chair, which was seen at the Museum of Modern Art.—ESTHER McCOY.

Left, this chair is of primavera laced with cord. Below left, in this chair designed for the house of Luis Barragan, Architect, the seat has been widened and the radius of the curve enlarged. It is in mahogany with webbing of hemp and ixtle.

The above chair is in mahogany and wicker and the frame is the same as the one which is laced with cord. It was designed for a home in Cuernavaca.

PHOTOGRAPHS: LOW COST CHAIRS, URSEL BERNATH
CLARA PORSET AND ALFONSO ROJAS, ELIZABETH TIMBERMAN
OTHER CHAIRS, LOLA ALVAREZ BRAVO

FIG. 13. "Chairs by Clara Porset," *Arts & Architecture*, July 1951

FIG. 14. Francisco Oller y Cestero (Puerto Rican, 1833–1917). *The Wake.* 1893. Oil on canvas, 8 × 13′ (240 × 400 cm).
MUSEUM OF HISTORY, ANTHROPOLOGY AND ART OF THE UNIVERSITY OF PUERTO RICO, RÍO PIEDRAS CAMPUS. The low-slung
butaque is seen to the right of the table.

FIG. 15. Diego Rivera (seated on a butaque), Frida Kahlo, and Aurora Reyes, 1943

its Mexican spirit because that is the effect she is looking for: she designs for Mexicans, Porset says, taking into account their characteristic physical traits, and seeks to produce forms that relate to their context and that come as close as possible to meeting their needs.[20] In the article, she notes that the majority of her furnishings are made by hand; the forms respond to tradition but also to the materials available and the skills of the artisans. This meant that production was limited and hence the costs were high. These aspects shed light on Porset's scarce production and why, with few exceptions, architects with large-budget projects were her principal clients.[21]

Iterations of the butaque are found throughout Mexico; the chair is now recognized as an essential part of the country's mestizo heritage. Anonymous and regional variants were developed, as were authorial versions by prominent designers [**FIGS. 14–16**].

FIG. 16. Francisco Zúñiga (Mexican, born Costa Rica. 1912–1998). *Evelia in a Butaque.* 1977. Charcoal and crayon on paper, 18 × 24½" (45.7 × 62.2 cm). HUDSON COUNTY COMMUNITY COLLEGE FOUNDATION

While Porset was not the first designer in Mexico to reconsider the butaque, she was the one who took the idea furthest, with profound reflections and decisive transformations. In the late 1930s designer William Spratling (born in the United States but based in Taxco, Guerrero) set up a carpentry and furniture studio where he produced and sold reinterpretations of colonial furnishings, such as clergymen's chairs and butaques, high tables with carved pedestals, and low tables with calfskin covers and forged-iron studs. Spratling made numerous versions of the butaque; some were lower and wider than the traditional form, others had an openwork heart on the upper part of the chair's back **[FIG. 17]**.

FIG. 17. William Spratling (Mexico-based, born USA. 1900–1967). Heart chair. c. 1940. Wood and cowhide, 31⁵⁄₁₆ × 20½ × 19½" (79.5 × 52 × 49.5 cm). COLECCIÓN CONSUELO + VIOLANTE ULRIC

Other designers who had settled in Mexico—such as Michael van Beuren with his San Miguelito and San Miguel chairs [FIGS. 18, 19], and Don Shoemaker with the Sloucher chair [FIG. 20]—created iterations of the butaque and integrated them into their commercial production lines. And native Mexican designers such as Alejandro Rangel Hidalgo [FIG. 21] and the architect Manuel Parra also borrowed from the butaque form to create iconic chairs in their own production. Throughout the twentieth century and into the twenty-first, many contemporary Mexican and Mexico-based designers have continued to turn to the butaque typology as a basis for playful, formal, and identitarian exercises with the aim of exploring a distinctively Mexican design—see for example works by

FIG. 18. Michael van Beuren (Mexico-based, born USA. 1911–2004). San Miguelito chair. c. 1947. Primavera wood and cotton fabric, 30 × 28¾ × 25½" (76 × 73 × 65 cm). COLECCIÓN JAN VAN BEUREN

FIG. 19. Michael van Beuren. San Miguel chair. c. 1947. Primavera wood and cotton fabric, 31⅞ × 37 × 38³⁄₁₆" (81 × 94 × 97 cm). COLECCIÓN JAN VAN BEUREN

FIG. 20. Don Shoemaker (Mexico-based, born USA. 1919–1990). Sloucher chair. c. 1960. Cocobolo wood and leather, 27 ⅛ × 22 ¹³⁄₁₆ × 27 ¹⁵⁄₁₆″ (69 × 58 × 71 cm). COLECCIÓN ALONSO DE GARAY

FIG. 21. Alejandro Rangel Hidalgo (Mexican, 1923–2000). Butaque Rangelino. n.d. Mahogany wood and cowhide, 24¹³⁄₁₆ × 31½ × 36⅝" (63 × 80 × 93 cm). COLLECTION THE MADRID CORDERO FAMILY

Fabien Cappello, Ricardo Casas, Laura Noriega, Juskani Alonso, and Moisés Hernández [**FIGS. 22–26**]. In other regions of the continent, designers such as the Venezuelan-Italian Bernardo Mazzei have created pieces in homage to Porset.

———

In 1952, with the support of Mexico City's Instituto Nacional de Bellas Artes, Porset organized her group show *El arte en la vida diaria: Exposición de objetos de buen diseño hechos en México*. The first formal design exhibition in a Mexican museum context, it was presented at two Mexico City venues: the Palacio de Bellas Artes in April 1952, and in the ground-floor classrooms of the recently inaugurated Ciudad Universitaria's school of philosophy and literature in October of the same year.

FIG. 22. Fabien Cappello (Mexican, born France 1984). Tropical chair. 2017. Metal, tule, and foam upholstered in cowhide with fur, 42 ⅛ × 27 ⁹⁄₁₆ × 24″ (107 × 70 × 61 cm). COLECCIÓN AGO PROJECTS. FABIEN CAPPELLO

FIG. 23. Ricardo Casas (Mexican, born 1979) for Notwaste. Clara chair. 2013. Oriented strand board (OSB) panel, cut with computer numerical control (CNC) and hand-sewn with rubber ingot, 29 ½ × 47 ¼ × 27 ½″ (75 × 120 × 70 cm). COLLECTION RICARDO CASAS

FIG. 24. Laura Noriega (Mexican, born 1980). Your Skin chair. 2012. Teak wood and fabric, 21 ¼ × 27 ½ × 27 ¹⁵⁄₁₆″ (54 × 70 × 71 cm). COLECCIÓN TRIBUTO

FIG. 25. Juskani Alonso (Mexican, born 1987). Tlayacapan chair. 2011. Pressed plywood, finished in oak with woven palm, 21 ⅝ × 23 ⅝ × 27 ½″ (55 × 60 × 70 cm). COLECCIÓN JUSKANI ALONSO

FIG. 26. Moisés Hernández (Mexican, born 1983) for Mexa. Clarita chair. 2022. Iron and fabric cord, 32 ¹¹⁄₁₆ × 36 ⅝ × 26″ (83 × 93 × 66.5 cm). COLECCIÓN MEXA

The exhibition articulated Porset's ideas about what modern Mexican design should be. Her intention was to show, as she had previously done in numerous articles, the best of the country's artisanal design and popular art, and their possible interactions with industrial design. She sought to identify and define principles of a modern national design, linked to the context and local work force anchored largely in artisanship and regional cultural conditions. At both venues, the exhibition was innovative from both a discursive and a museological standpoint. The walls were hung with huge photographs made by Lola Álvarez Bravo, showing artisans in their work settings: displayed in a manner inspired by the innovative exhibition designs of Bauhaus artist Herbert Bayer, the images helped to create an immersive visual experience [FIG. 27]. For the exhibition, Porset brought together complete modern industrial kitchens and traditional domestic objects. The display of the various elements struck a tone between a department store showroom and a museum space [FIG. 28].

FIG. 27. Installation view of *El arte en la vida diaria: Exposición de objetos de buen diseño hechos en México*, Palacio de Bellas Artes, Mexico City, 1952

FIG. 28. Installation view of *El arte en la vida diaria: Exposición de objetos de buen diseño hechos en México,*
Ciudad Universitaria, UNAM, Mexico City, 1952

FIG. 29. Installation view of *Machine Art*, The Museum of Modern Art, New York, 1934

FIG. 30. Installation view of *El arte en la vida diaria: Exposición de objetos de buen diseño hechos en México,* Palacio de Bellas Artes, Mexico City, 1952

The presentation of the show seems clearly to have been influenced by *Machine Art* [**FIG. 29**], the radical exhibition held at MoMA in 1934 that brought focus to the aesthetic qualities of industrially produced objects (and which Porset may well have seen during her visit to the United States that year). Despite the nods to the MoMA exhibition, however, Porset insisted that *El arte en la vida diaria* was grounded in local territory and culture by, for example, placing traditional *equipales* seating from Michoacán at strategic rest spots, for visitors' use—effectively eliminating the distance between a formal exhibition experience and corporeal seduction. The show also included diagrams with wire figures and texts analyzing the physical act of sitting down: a thorough brief for popular ergonomics [**FIG. 30**]. And in the accompanying exhibition catalogue (designed by the Spanish artist Miguel Prieto, exiled from his home country and living in Mexico), Porset illustrated her research on the butaque with images of a traditional chair and of the version she was proposing.

RETURN TO CUBA: DISILLUSIONMENT AND NEW PATHS

Fidel Castro was sworn in as prime minister of Cuba in 1959. Porset, who had visited Cuba in the late 1940s to deliver a series of lectures at the Universidad de La Habana [FIG. 31], was now invited to relocate to her native land to help "design" the country's revolution. In 1962 she closed her Mexico City studio and returned, somewhat starry-eyed, to her homeland. Over the next years, her husband Xavier Guerrero shuttled between Mexico and Cuba; both of them were convinced that the revolutionary cause warranted this change in their lives.

Castro, aware of the need to improve the living conditions of the island's people, commissioned numerous projects from Porset. With Guerrero, she designed and built the furniture for the Ciudad Escolar Camilo Cienfuegos, with a student body of five thousand [FIG. 32]. She undertook the furniture designs for Cuba's national schools of modern dance and visual arts (built by the architect Ricardo Porro in 1961), as well as furnishings for the rectory of the Universidad de La Habana in 1962. She was also asked to create Cuba's first school of industrial design, encouraged personally by Ernesto "Che" Guevara.[22]

The Ciudad Escolar Camilo Cienfuegos education complex, inaugurated in 1960 in Cuba's Sierra Maestra, was a major endeavor that had been initiated during the revolution. The furniture designs for the complex presented a challenge to Porset and Guerrero, but also a pleasure, in that the Ciudad Escolar signaled a utopia realized at long last. In Mexico Porset had undertaken various exercises designing furnishings for workers, projects that in the end had disappointed her.[23] For the Camilo Cienfuegos complex, she and Guerrero adapted the rural furnishings that they had developed in 1941 to the conditions on the island. Porset also revisited designs she had begun a decade before, in the early 1950s, for the Casa Campesina in Veracruz (a collaboration with the architect Alberto T. Arai)—now modifying her original ideas to create a set of furniture using Cuban varieties of wood and techniques used by local artisans, whom she hired to work on the project.

In the late 1940s, as Porset was planning *El arte en la vida diaria* in Mexico City, she had proposed an ambitious project to Fernando Gamboa, director of the visual arts department at Mexico's Instituto Nacional de Bellas Artes: a school of design that would promote dialogues between artisanship and industry, popular art and design.[24] Porset furthered these ideas in Cuba in the early 1960s, formulating a design program that would engage the island's popular culture, revalorize the work of artisans, and bring new ideas and energy to industrial design. In 1962 she initiated plans for the Escuela Superior de Diseño Industrial, a school that would offer both technical and professional design courses. It would operate under the auspices of Cuba's Ministerio de Industrias, then directed by Che Guevara. Seeking models for the institution's curriculum, Porset made a research trip to design schools in Moscow, Stockholm, Warsaw, Prague, Weimar,

FIG. 31. Clara Porset arriving in Cuba, c. 1948

FIG. 32. Xavier Guerrero with a set of children's chairs designed by Guerrero and Clara Porset for Ciudad Escolar Camilo Cienfuegos, Cuba, c. 1961–62

and Halle.[25] Soon after, in 1965, she inaugurated the design program for the ministry, which was located in the Havana neighborhood of Reparto Siboney. Ultimately, however, the Escuela Superior de Diseño Industrial could maintain only the technical end of its education program, and Porset's dream of training workers and professionals in design in Cuba was cut short.

Disheartened and disillusioned, she decided to return to Mexico. In a letter Porset wrote to friends in 1977, her sadness is evident:

> I feel more alone than ever. How can it be that Clarita Porset should die away from her country? I'm capable of writing Fidel and reminding him that I was the one who made the first Cuban furnishings in the Sierra Maestra . . . I don't think he's forgotten about me . . . nor that I personally gave him the furniture for that extraordinary school. Nor do I think he's forgotten about . . . my attempt with Che to create a school of industrial design.[26]

Once back in Mexico, Porset chose a dual professional path of design and education. She joined the teaching staff of the Centro de Investigaciones de Diseño Industrial (CIDI: Center for Research on Industrial Design) at the Universidad Nacional Autónoma de México's school of architecture. There, alongside another distinguished designer, Horacio Durán, she founded the undergraduate course in industrial design [FIG. 33]. After the death of Guerrero in 1974, Porset turned away from design to dedicate herself fully to teaching until her death, in Mexico City, in 1981.

In her will, Porset stipulated that her library and archive should be housed at the CIDI (where they may be consulted to this day), and that her house should be sold to create a fund to provide designers with financial support to study abroad.[27] In 2004 the directors of the CIDI established the Premio Clara Porset, a prize awarded every two years, the aim of which is to confer greater visibility on the work of female students and women who have recently entered the field of design professionally.

Porset's intensive work with the butaque, one of her signature achievements, is in itself an important cultural bequest. She understood and demonstrated the significance of context—both geographic and cultural—to the work of the designer. Finally, she was an early champion of the notion that artisanal products and popular art can engage in dialogue with industrial design, a concept central to Mexico's contribution to the modernist project.

FIG. 33. Clara Porset and Horacio Durán (left of Porset) with faculty and students from the undergraduate industrial design program of the Facultad de Arquitectura at UNAM, c. 1969

NOTES

1. Clara Porset, "¿Qué es diseño?," *Arquitectura México*, no. 28 (1949): 168–73.

2. MoMA presented a number of exhibitions with a view to establishing a canon of "good design," among them *Machine Art* (1934) and *Useful Household Objects under $5* (1938), followed by *Useful Objects of American Design under $10* (1939–40). The "useful objects" exhibitions were so popular that they ran as an annual series for nine years (although by 1947 the top price had increased to $100).

3. Henri Rapin was an architect, illustrator, and decorator; he was part of the organizing team of the 1925 Exposition Internationale des Arts Décoratifs et Industriels Modernes in Paris.

4. The Grupo Minorista was made up of artists and intellectuals who championed anti-imperialism and advocated for social causes and the creation of a national culture in Cuba.

5. For more on the Lyceum de La Habana, see Rosario Rexach, "El Lyceum de La Habana como institución cultural," in *Actas del IX Congreso de la Asociación Internacional de Hispanistas 18–23 agosto 1986*, vol. 2 (Berlin: Vervuert, 1989), 679–90; cervantesvirtual.com/nd/ark:/59851/bmct1713; and Whigman Montoya Deler, *El Lyceum y Lawn Tennis Club: Su huella en la cultura cubana* (Houston, TX: Ediciones Laponia, 2022).

6. For a more in-depth look at Porset's political ideas, as well as her trajectory and personal relationships associated with political beliefs, see Randal Sheppard, "Clara Porset in Mid-Twentieth-Century Mexico: The Politics of Designing, Producing, and Consuming Revolutionary Nationalist Modernity," *Americas* 75, no. 2 (2018): 349–79. I am grateful to Dr. Sheppard for his invaluable support of my research.

7. See Marguerite Young, "Exiled in New York," *Pittsburgh Press*, May 7, 1933.

8. "Young Woman Revolutionary Sees Cubans Achieving Aims Now; Aristocrat Who Had to Flee for Life Pleads for Tolerant View," *Stevens Point Journal*, September 25, 1933; Leslie Eiche, "The World at a Glance," *Brownsville Herald*, September 16, 1933.

9. For more on the postrevolutionary national project associated with culture, design, and crafts, see Rick A. López, *Crafting Mexico: Intellectuals, Artisans, and the State after the Revolution* (Durham, NC: Duke University Press, 2010).

10. Xavier Guerrero was a cultured and well-educated artist, part of the group that organized the 1921 Exposición de Artes Populares, an important moment in the history of design and popular art in Mexico. In 1922 author and cultural promotor Katherine Anne Porter proposed a second iteration of this show to travel to the United States, specifically to Los Angeles. Guerrero was a curator of the latter exposition and also one of its principal organizers. For more on this show, see Karen Cordero Reiman, "Fuentes para una historia social del 'arte popular' mexicano: 1920–1950," *Memoria, Museo Nacional de Arte* 2 (Spring–Summer, 1990): 31–55; Alicia Azuela de la Cueva, "Las artes plásticas en las conmemoraciones de los centenarios de la Independencia, 1910, 1921," in *Asedios a los centenarios (1910 y 1921)*, ed. Virginia Guedea (Mexico City: Fondo de Cultura Económica, 2010), 108–65; and Mireida Velázquez Torres, "'The Profound and Touching Expression of a Very Old Race': Katherine Anne Porter y la Exposición de Arte Popular Mexicano de 1922" (presentation at the Third International Forum for Emerging Scholars: Synchronicity: Contacts and Divergences in Latin American and U.S. Latino Art [19th Century to the Present], University of Texas at Austin, October 2012); academia.edu/8773211/Katherine_Anne_Porter_y_la_Exposici%C3%B3n_de_Arte_Popular_Mexicano_de_1922.

11. Among Guerrero and Porset's later collaborations were furniture designs for architect Enrique Gebhard in Santiago de Chile (1948), and school furniture designs in Cuba's Sierra Maestra (1960).

12. Porset made this point clear in her lecture "La decoración interior contemporánea: Su adaptación al trópico," at the Auditórium de La Habana on May 22, 1931, repr. in Jorge R. Bermúdez, *Clara Porset: Diseño y cultura* (Havana: Editorial Letras Cubanas, 2005), 67–82.

13. Clara Porset, "Folk Furniture of Mexico," *School Arts Magazine* 47, no. 5 (January 1948): 161–67.

14. The popularity of Mexico during this era is explored in Helen Delpar, *The Enormous Vogue of Things Mexican: Cultural Relations between the United States and Mexico, 1920–1935* (Tuscaloosa: University Alabama Press, 1995).

15. Porset, a member of the Communist Party and of the Frente de Liberación Nacional, followed a line of discourse regarding popular art and cultural identity in Mexico that had been developed—with variants—over the previous two decades by Mexican intellectuals and artists including her husband, Xavier Guerrero, along with anthropologist Manuel Gamio, and painters Dr. Atl, Roberto Montenegro, and Gabriel Fernández Ledesma, among others.

16. Porset, "Folk Furniture of Mexico."

17. The construction of the Pan-American Highway, the promotion of cultural tourism in Mexico by authors such as Anita Brenner and magazines addressed to foreigners such as *Mexican Life*, as well as the publication of numerous tourist and shopping guides all helped fuel this interest.

18. Mary Roche, "Furniture Depicts Different Mexico," *New York Times*, Feburary 4, 1947.

19. Jorge Rivas Pérez, "Butacas y butaques: Sillas nuevas para el Nuevo Mundo," in *Silla mexicana*, ed. Ana Elena Mallet (Mexico City: Arquine/Secretaría de Cultura, 2018), 36.

20. "Chairs by Clara Porset," *Arts & Architecture* 68, no. 7 (July 1951): 34–35.

21. Porset was extremely interested in "social design"—that is, design intended to improve the well-being of communities. Porset's social design projects include her collaborations with the architect Mario Pani in 1947 for the interiors of the Centro Urbano Presidente Alemán, and with the architect Alberto T. Arai for the Casa Campesina by the Papaloapan River in 1952. During the 1960s, following her return to Cuba, she and Guerrero designed the furnishings for the Ciudad Escolar Camilo Cienfuegos in the Sierra Maestra.

22. See Óscar Salinas Flores, *Clara Porset: Una vida inquieta, una obra sin igual* (Mexico City: UNAM, Facultad de Arquitectura, 2001), 59.

23. In Mexico, Porset took on various jobs designing low-cost furniture for government workers. However, the Centro Urbano Presidente Alemán project in Mexico City, carried out between 1947 and 1949 with the architect Mario Pani, disappointed her. In a text published in the journal *Espacios* (no. 16), in 1953, she confessed her disenchantment with Mexico's impoverished culture of design and what she saw as the failure of the furniture and interior design project.

24. In an undated letter to Fernando Gamboa, Porset proposes the exhibition *El arte en la vida diaria: Exposición de objetos de buen diseño hechos en México*, along with a complete program that involved having a gallery of "art in daily life" at Mexico City's Museo de Arte Moderno (then in the planning stages) and a school of design. The letter is housed in the Archivo Clara Porset Dumas, Centro de Investigaciones de Diseño Industrial, Facultad de Arquitectura, UNAM.

25. Salinas Flores, *Clara Porset*, 59.

26. Porset, 1977 letter to friends identified only as "Ada" and "Beba," in ibid., 40.

27. From this fund, two Clara Porset grants were awarded initially, in 1984 and 1985. The biennial Premio Clara Porset was instituted in 2004. As of 2023, twenty prizes had been awarded.

FOR FURTHER READING

Aste, Richard, ed. *Behind Closed Doors: Art in the Spanish American Home, 1492–1898.* Exh. cat. New York: Brooklyn Museum, Monacelli Press, 2013. See esp. Jorge Rivas Pérez, "Domestic Display in the Spanish Overseas Territories," 49–103.

Kaplan, Wendy, ed. *Design in California and Mexico, 1915–1985: Found in Translation.* Exh. cat. Los Angeles: Los Angeles County Museum of Art; New York: Prestel, 2017.

Pierce, Donna, ed. *Festivals & Daily Life in the Arts of Colonial Latin America, 1492–1850: Papers from the 2012 Mayer Center Symposium at the Denver Art Museum.* Denver: Denver Art Museum, 2014. See esp. Jorge Rivas Pérez, "Transforming Status: The Genesis of the New World Butaca," 111–28.

Rangel, Gabriela, and Jorge Rivas Pérez, eds. *Moderno: Design for Living in Brazil, Mexico, and Venezuela, 1940–1978.* Exh. cat. New York: Americas Society, 2015.

Ryan, Zoë, ed. *In a Cloud, in a Wall, in a Chair: Six Modernists in Mexico at Midcentury.* Exh. cat. Chicago: Art Institute of Chicago, 2019. See esp. Randal Sheppard, "Clara Porset and the Politics of Design," 77–89; Christina L. De León, "A Friendship Formed by a Chair: Clara Porset and Esther McCoy," 91–100; and plates, 101–17.

Published to accompany the exhibition
Crafting Modernity: Design in Latin America, 1940–1980
at The Museum of Modern Art, New York,
March 8–September 22, 2024

Produced by the Department of Publications,
The Museum of Modern Art, New York

Hannah Kim, Business and Marketing Director
Joseph Mohan, Production Director
Curtis R. Scott, Associate Publisher

Edited by Diana C. Stoll
Series designed by Miko McGinty and Rita Jules
Layout by Athina Fili
Production by Matthew Pimm
Proofread by Sophie Golub
Printed and bound by Ofset Yapımevi, Istanbul

The essay by Ana Elena Mallet was translated from the
Spanish by Christopher Winks.

Typeset in Ideal Sans
Printed on 150 gsm Magno Satin

Published by The Museum of Modern Art
11 West 53 Street
New York, NY 10019-5497
www.moma.org

ISBN: 978-1-63345-162-9

Distributed in the United States and Canada by
ARTBOOK | D.A.P.
75 Broad Street, Suite 630
New York, NY 10004
www.artbook.com

Distributed outside the United States and Canada by
Thames & Hudson
181A High Holborn
London WC1V 7QX
www.thamesandhudson.com

Printed and bound in Turkey